I'm Reading Abou

ALABAMA

The Yellowhammer State!

by Carole Marsh

Alabama is a great state.
It is one of a kind.

What makes Alabama special?
Let's read about it
and see!

Let's go!

Who lived in Alabama first?

Native Americans did!

They moved around to find food.
They hunted in Alabama's woods.
They fished in Alabama's rivers.
They gathered fruits and seeds and nuts.

Native Americans lived off the land.

Like me!

4

EXPLORERS

Explorers came to Alabama in 1540.
They came from the country of Spain.

Hernando de Soto was their leader.
He and his men were looking for cities of gold!

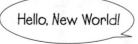
Hello, New World!

SETTLEMENT

French explorers came to Alabama.
They built a settlement.
They called it Mobile.

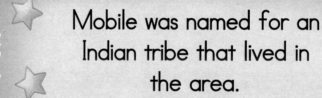

Mobile was named for an
Indian tribe that lived in
the area.

That looks like a
nice place to live!

8

Mobile

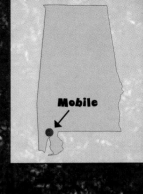
Mobile

Site de
Vieux Mobile
Fort Louis de la Louisiane Première
Capitale de la Louisiane Française
1702-1711
Fondée par
Pierre Le Moyne d'Iberville
par ordre de Louis XIV, Roi de France
Érigée par Colonial Dames XVII Century
29 Septembre, 2001

STATEHOOD

Alabama was the 22nd state
to join the United States of America!

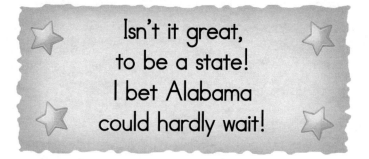

Isn't it great,
to be a state!
I bet Alabama
could hardly wait!

Alabama became a state in 1819.

I am the state flag.
I was adopted in 1895.

What colors am I?
Red. White.

Look at me.
What else do you see?

I fly high over the state of Alabama!

Salute!

12

Say hello to Montgomery,
the capital city of Alabama!

There is an important building in Montgomery.
It is the State Capitol.
Alabama's governor and many
important people work there!

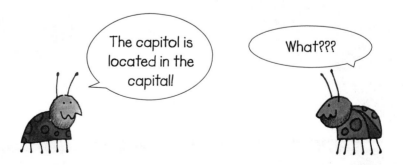

The capitol is located in the capital!

What???

Capitol

Montgomery

Capital

I am a seal,
but I am not the State Seal.
If I were, I would be very important.
I would be stamped on many official papers.
(Ouch, that might hurt!)

NICKNAME

State nicknames are fun!
State nicknames are great!
They share fun facts
about each state!

Alabama has several nicknames.
One nickname is "The Yellowhammer State."

The Yellowhammer is a woodpecker!

Look at Alabama.
Alabama is in a region called "the South."

Alabama borders four other states.
Find them on the map!

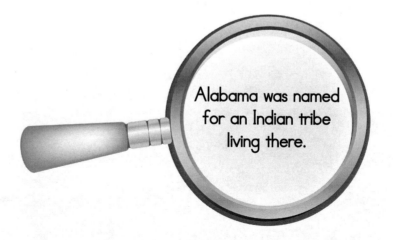

Alabama was named
for an Indian tribe
living there.

COUNTIES

Alabama is divided into 67 counties.
Counties are a form of local government.
Counties provide services that people need!
Those services include:

Schools　　**Parks**　　**Libraries**　　**Police**

Firefighters　　　　**and More!**

Counties

ALABAMA'S CAPITAL, MONTGOMERY, IS IN MONTGOMERY COUNTY.

Many famous People

PEOPLE

Booker T. Washington
Teacher who founded the Tuskegee Institute

George Washington Carver
Scientist who greatly improved farming in the South

Rosa Parks
Known as the "Mother of the Civil Rights Movement"

Call our state home!

Let's hang out!

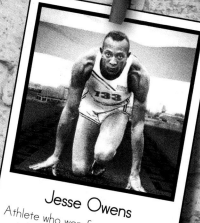

Jesse Owens
Athlete who won four gold medals
at the 1936 Summer Olympics

Condoleezza Rice
First female African American
U.S. Secretary of State

Mae Jemison
First female African
American astronaut

25

I am the state bird, and I fly
over Alabama, proud and high.

As I fly, up in the sky,
I flap my wings to tell you "Hi!"

The Alabama state bird is the Yellowhammer.

Camellia

I am the Camellia.
I am the state flower.

I can grow in sunny or shady places.
I bloom from early fall to late spring!
I help make Alabama beautiful!

Look at me! Smell me!
My flowers are usually
white, pink, or red!

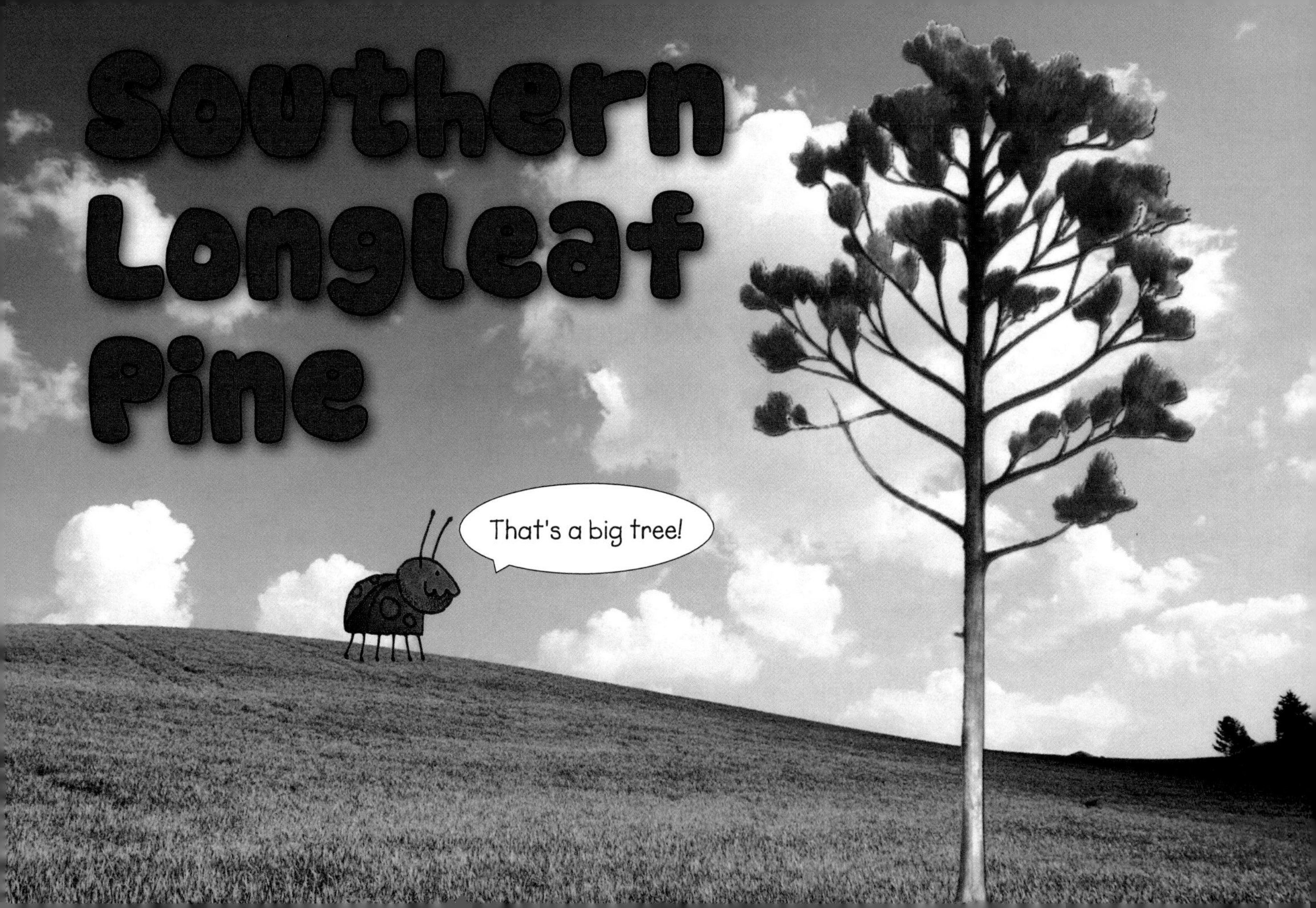
Southern Longleaf Pine
That's a big tree!

I am a Southern Longleaf Pine—I'm the state tree.
Central and southern Alabama
is where to find me.

My roots run deep, they keep me strong.
My pine needles are about 12 inches long!

I stand up straight, big and tall.
Don't climb too high—it would hurt to fall!

Monarch Butterfly

I am the Monarch Butterfly.
I am the state insect.

I flit and I fly from flower to flower.
I am looking for nectar to drink.

Look at my beautiful wings.
What colors do you see?

Let's go to the beach!

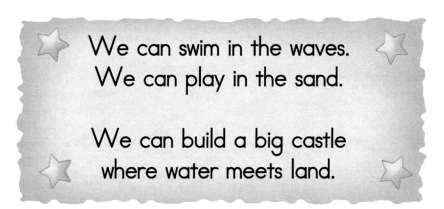

We can swim in the waves.
We can play in the sand.

We can build a big castle
where water meets land.

Alabama's beaches are home to many animals:

Sea Turtles   **Birds**   **Crabs**   **Dolphins**   **and More!**

BEACHES

Alabama's mountains
are the place to be.
Hiking, fishing, camping—
fun for you and me.

If you were to climb
to the top of a tree,
you might be able to see Tennessee!

Alabama's highest point is Cheaha Mountain.

MOUNTAINS

Alabama has many rivers.
People like to use rivers for
boating and fishing!

This habitat is home to many animals:

Birds **Deer** **Snakes** **Frogs** **Fish** **and More!**

Many of Alabama's early
settlers built towns along rivers.

RIVERS

USS Alabama

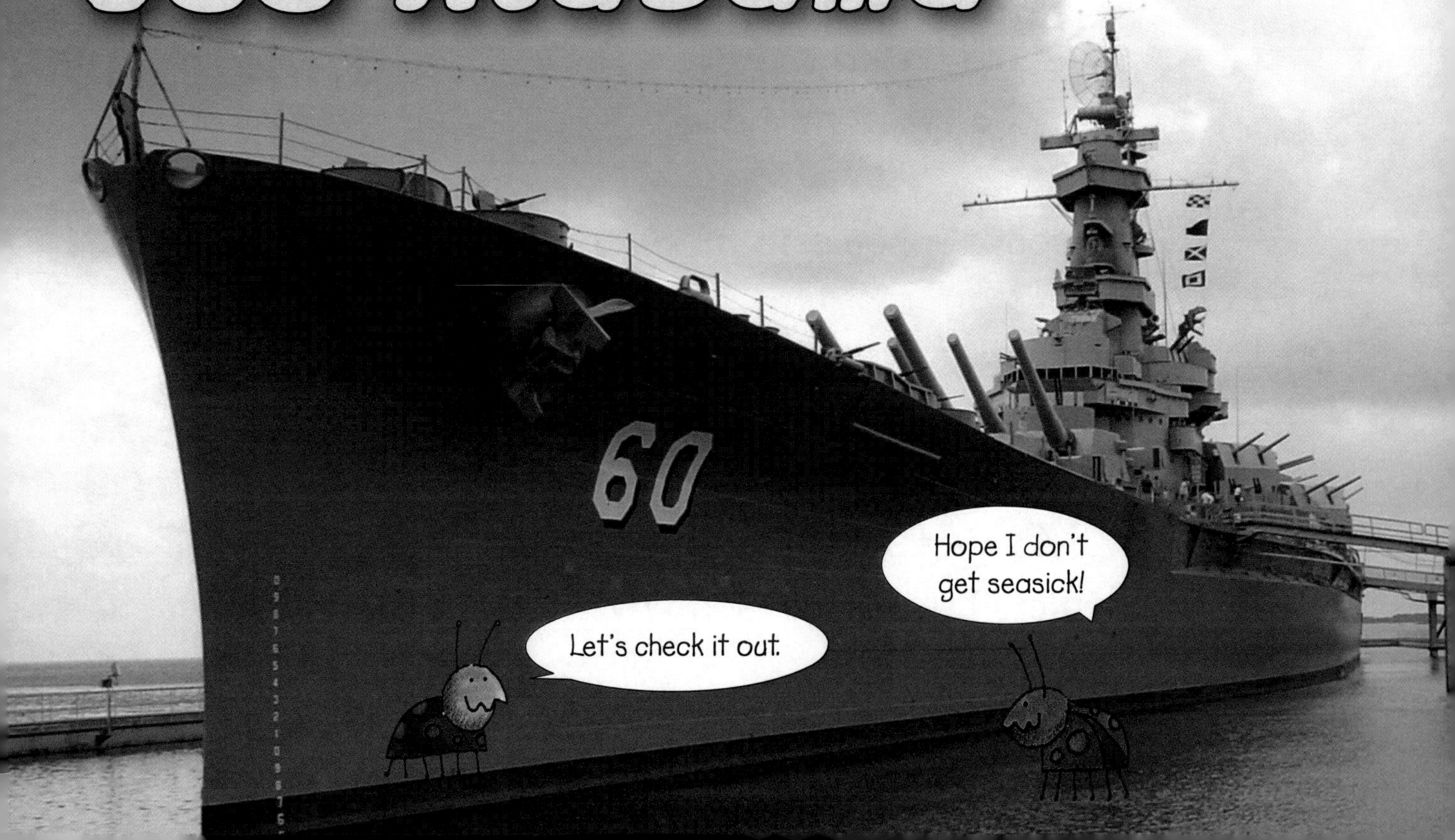

A huge warship sits in Mobile Bay.
It is named the USS *Alabama*.
That ship carried American sailors in World War II.
Today, visitors can go onto the ship and explore it!

The USS *Alabama's* nickname
is the "Lucky A."

Alabama has many farms.
Why?
Because Alabama has good soil and a warm climate!

Some of the top crops grown in Alabama are:

Cotton Peanuts Corn Soybeans

Hey!
Don't forget about me!
I am a young chicken.
They call me a "broiler."
Alabama raises lots of broilers!

Sports in Alabama

Baseball! Basketball! Football!
Alabama has it all.

Whether you like to watch or play,
You are sure to have a ball!

Crimson Tide   Tigers

Trojans

See you at the
Talladega Superspeedway!

& More!

Alabama: Home of U.S. Space & Rocket Center

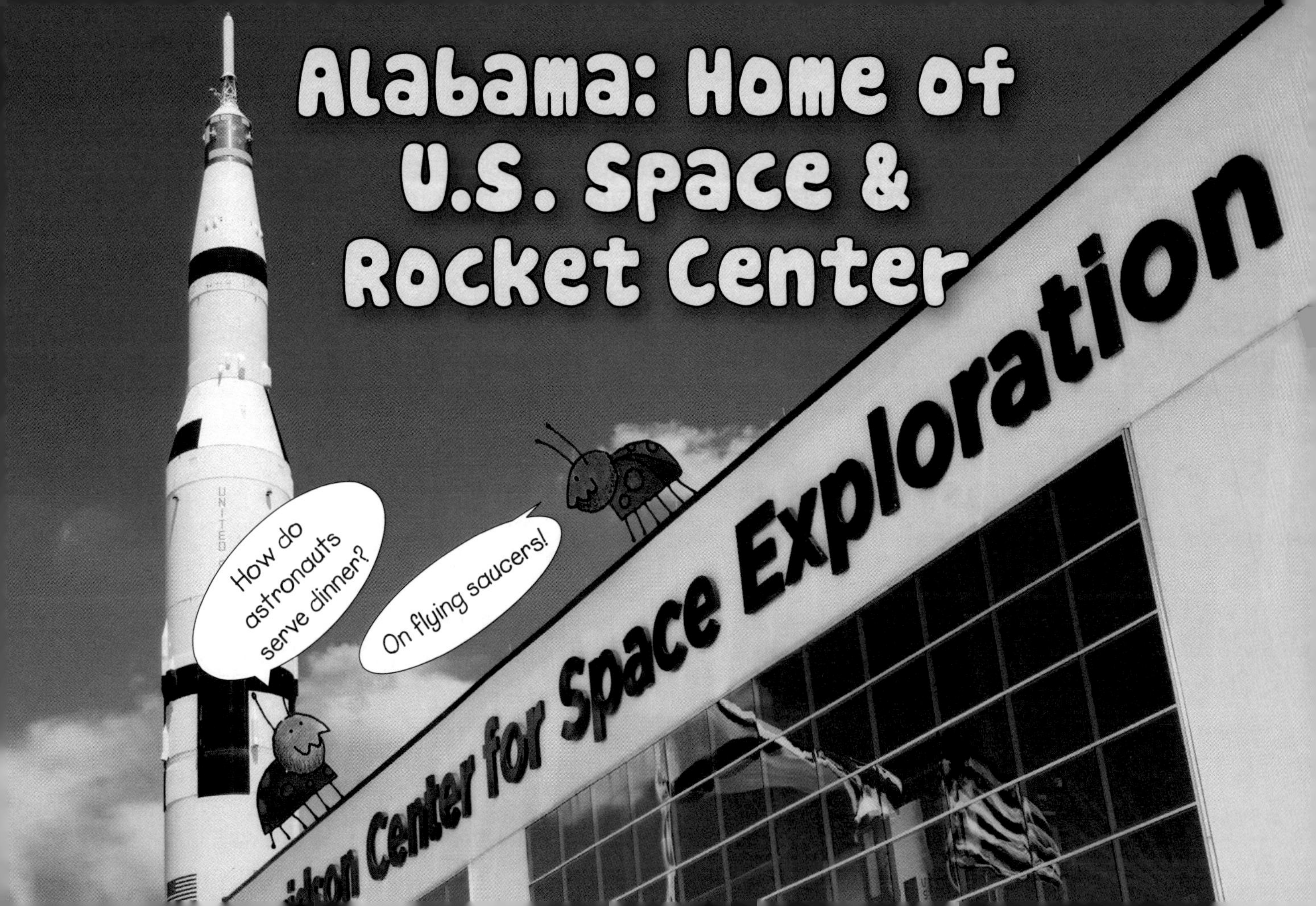

The U.S. Space & Rocket Center is in Huntsville.
It is a museum all about space.
Visitors can see rockets, spacecraft,
and other space items!

Kids can go to Space Camp at
the Space & Rocket Center!

GLOSSARY

astronaut: a person trained to travel in a spacecraft

climate: weather conditions in an area over a long period of time

habitat: a place where plants or animals naturally live

local: related to a town or small area, rather than a big city or large area

museum: a building people can visit to see interesting and valuable things

nectar: a sweet liquid produced by plants, especially flowers

region: an area that has similar characteristics

rocket: a long, round device that is launched into the air

settlement: the first community in an area

woodpecker: a bird with a strong beak that it hammers into trees to find insects